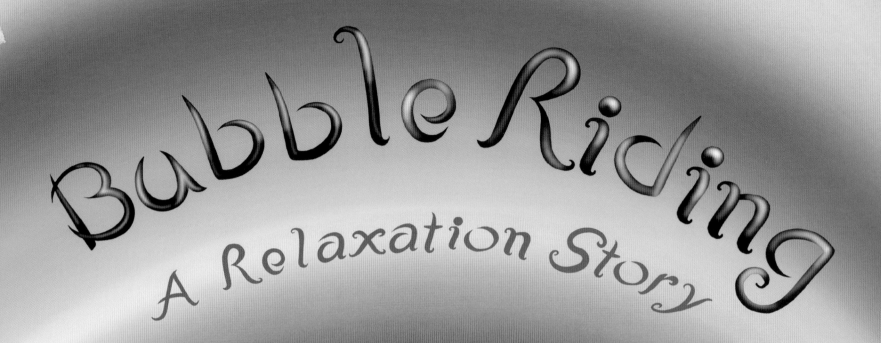

Bubble Riding

A Relaxation Story

by Lori Lite
illustrated by Max Stasyuk

Copyright 2008 Lori Lite

Collect the Indigo Dreams Series and watch your whole family manage anxiety, stress and anger…

CD/Audio Books:

Indigo Dreams

Indigo Ocean Dreams

Indigo Teen Dreams

Indigo Dreams:
Garden of Wellness

Indigo Dreams:
Adult Relaxation

Indigo Dreams:
3 CD Set

Books:

The Goodnight Caterpillar

A Boy and a Turtle

Bubble Riding

Angry Octopus

Sea Otter Cove

Affirmation Weaver

A Boy and a Bear

The Affirmation Web

Curriculum Kits:

Children's Wellness Curriculum

Children's Stress Awareness Curriculum

**Books, CDs, curriculums, and other products designed
to empower children, teens, and adults are available at
www.StressFreeKids.com**

Congratulations!

You are going to read a story called *Bubble Riding*. It is fun to pretend that you are the sea child or that you are the turtle as you imagine or visualize the colors of the rainbow. Notice how the colors feel!

A sea child just finished her long day. She was up early for school and worked very hard learning new things. She went to swim class and played with her friends. Every day was busy for her and she felt very tired and tense.

She was proud of all the things she had accomplished for the day and decided to treat herself to her favorite game. She was sure that she was the only one in the entire ocean that knew how to play. After all, she was the one who made up the game she called Bubble Riding.

She swished her strong tail and swam to the edge of the coral reef. This is where she would find a water spout on the bottom of the ocean floor. As she swam closer she could feel the water getting warmer and warmer. She could see the tiny bubbles lifting through the sand and swaying back and forth in the current. The bubbles meant that she had found her water spout. The sea child sat still and focused on the bubbles. She knew that if she was patient, a bubble big enough to ride would come her way.

After a few moments a large bubble emerged from the spout. She hugged the bubble and felt the bubble wrap itself around her like a pair of loving arms. The sea child was now cradled inside the warm, safe bubble.

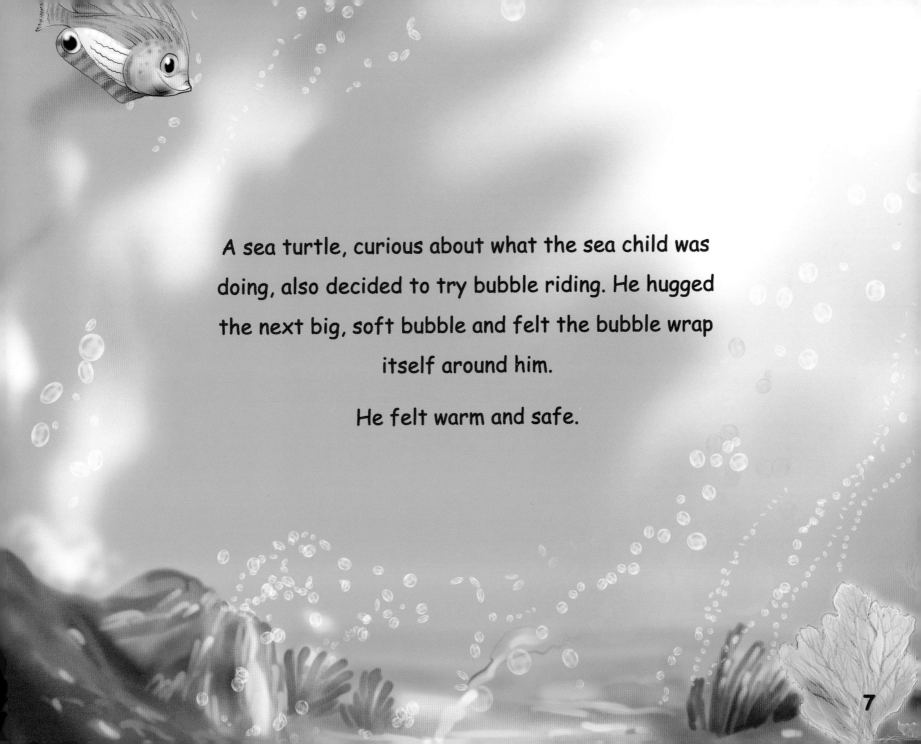

A sea turtle, curious about what the sea child was doing, also decided to try bubble riding. He hugged the next big, soft bubble and felt the bubble wrap itself around him.

He felt warm and safe.

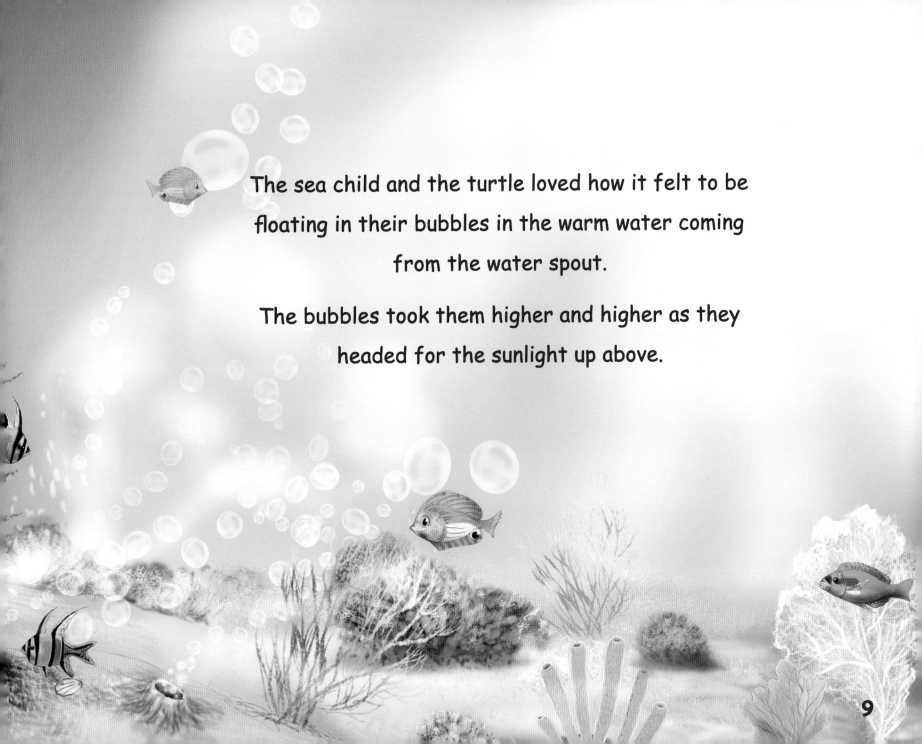

The sea child and the turtle loved how it felt to be floating in their bubbles in the warm water coming from the water spout.

The bubbles took them higher and higher as they headed for the sunlight up above.

The sea child noticed a beautiful rainbow stretching from the sky above all the way down through the ocean to the coral below her.

She shut her eyes and imagined that the colors of the rainbow that filled the ocean could also fill her bubble.

The color red touched the edge of the sea child's bubble and poured into the space around her.

She imagined that the color red was flowing into her tail allowing her to feel energized and healthy.

The red kept moving slowly as it warmed her stomach and chest. It poured into her arms... cascading down to her finger tips. The red explored her neck and face and swirled around her head leaving her mind quiet and still.

She was floating in a sea of red.

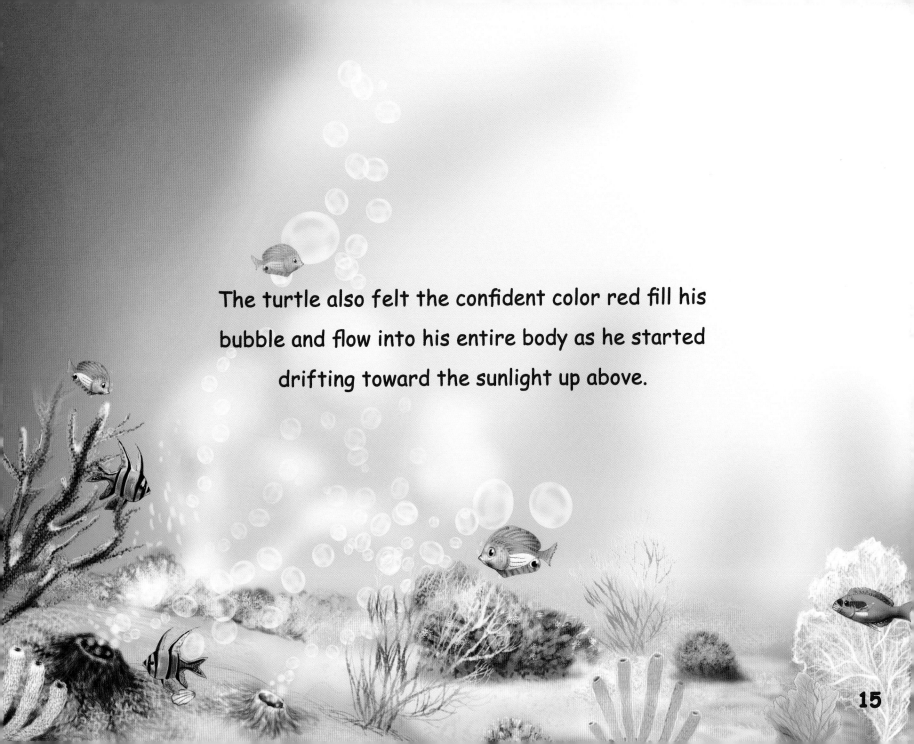

The turtle also felt the confident color red fill his bubble and flow into his entire body as he started drifting toward the sunlight up above.

The color orange touched the edge of the sea child's bubble and poured into the space around her.

She imagined that the color orange was flowing into her tail allowing her to feel happy as she let go of all her tightness.

The orange moved slowly as it warmed her stomach and chest. It poured into her arms...cascading down to her finger tips. The orange explored her neck and face and swirled around her head leaving her mind quiet and still.

She was floating in a sea of orange.

The turtle also felt the happy color orange fill his bubble and flow into his entire body as he drifted toward the sunlight up above.

The color yellow touched the edge of the sea child's bubble and poured into the space around her.

She imagined that the color yellow was flowing into her tail allowing her to feel an inner glow.

The yellow moved slowly as it warmed her stomach and chest. It poured into her arms... cascading down to her finger tips. The yellow explored her neck and face and swirled around her head leaving her mind quiet and still.

She was floating in a sea of yellow.

The turtle also felt the golden color yellow fill his
bubble and flow into his entire body as he drifted
closer to the sunlight up above.

The color green touched the edge of the sea child's bubble and poured into the space around her.

She imagined that the color green was flowing into her tail allowing her to feel love.

The green moved slowly as it warmed her stomach and chest. It poured into her arms...cascading down to her finger tips. The green explored her neck and face and swirled around her head leaving her mind quiet and still.

She was floating in a sea of green.

The turtle also felt the loving color green fill his bubble and flow into his entire body as he drifted even closer to the sunlight up above.

27

The color blue touched the edge of the sea child's bubble and poured into the space around her.

She imagined that the color blue was flowing into her tail allowing her to relax and see things differently.

The blue moved slowly as it warmed her stomach and chest. It poured into her arms...cascading down to her finger tips. The blue explored her neck and face and swirled around her head leaving her mind quiet and still.

She was floating in a sea of blue.

The turtle also felt the calming color blue fill his
bubble and flow into his entire body as he drifted
still closer to the sunlight up above.

The color purple touched the edge of the sea child's bubble and poured into the space around her.

She imagined that the color purple was flowing into her tail allowing her to feel peaceful and clear.

The purple moved slowly as it warmed her stomach and chest. It poured into her arms...cascading down to her finger tips. The purple explored her neck and face and swirled around her head leaving her mind quiet and still.

She was floating in a sea of purple.

The turtle also felt the peaceful color purple fill his
bubble and flow into his entire body.
They both drifted so close to the sunlight that
all the colors and feelings of the rainbow mixed
with the warm rays of the sun.

As the colors mixed, they became whiter and whiter until the sea child and the turtle found themselves embraced by a blanket of pure, white light. Their bubbles rocked them both back and forth as they enjoyed the soothing white glow. Together the rainbow and the loving arms of their bubbles helped them to feel balanced and calm.

They both knew that they had experienced the wonder of colors!